YOU ARE...

THIRTY NAMES GOD HAS GIVEN YOU AND WHAT THEY MEAN

MICHELLE KEENER

Woodside Books

Soli Deo Gloria

INTRODUCTION

We live in a world of labels. We have warning labels on everything from diapers to curling irons, lists of ingredients we can't
pronounce on our favorite snack foods, and words we carelessly
slap on each other and ourselves. Smart, foolish, skinny, fat, stay-
at-home mom, working mother, has-it-all-together, hot mess.

All too often we accept these adjectives, carrying them like
baggage, like a prison sentence from our past, building these
words into walls that blot out our hopes and suffocate our
dreams. For too long we have embraced these labels, tattooed
them on our heart, used them to wallpaper our souls, and let
them play on an endless loop through our minds.

"Who am I to think I can do that?"

"I'm not smart enough or talented enough."

"I'm uneducated."

"What if I fail?"

"People will laugh at me."

"I'm too busy."

"I have nothing to offer."

Those words can be paralyzing. They can keep us stuck in fear, shame, or worry, making us too afraid to step into the life God has called us to.

But what if none of it is true?

What if none of the labels we have accepted and none of the words the world has spoken over us are true? What if God has been trying to tell us who we really are and we've been too busy listening to the world to hear His voice?

My friend, God knows *you*. He knows you personally. He knows your past, your present, and your future. He knows the plans He has for you, the gifts He has chosen for you, and the work He has set aside for you. He knows your hopes and your dreams, your deepest secrets and your greatest wounds. He has been with you every day of your life, and He will never leave you.

God never lies. When He tells you that you are loved…you are. When He tells you that you are treasured…you are. When He says that you are called…you are. The world will lie to you. We may even lie to ourselves, but God will always tell us the truth. When He says something, it is absolutely, one-hundred percent true. So, if God says you are His…you are.

When we take off the labels the world has given us, when we lay aside the words we have given ourselves and accept what God says about us, we can step into the destiny He has planned for us. We will begin to walk in the power of His truth, letting it wash over us, refreshing us, and giving us confidence to walk in the light of His love and grace.

Over the next thirty days we'll look at who God says you are. His words are trustworthy and true. I encourage you to embrace these names, knowing that God has written them on your heart. Believe the truth of God's word, accept what He says about you and let His love for you banish any other labels that have been stuck on your life. God wants you to live as His precious, chosen, gifted child. That begins when you believe that you are who God says you are.

YOU ARE LOVED

"I have loved you with an everlasting love."
Jeremiah 31:3

If you have ever had your heart broken, you know that in this world love can be fleeting. People may love you one day, but not the next. Love feels uncertain instead of lasting and unconditional. People who have promised to love each other for the rest of their lives may end up in divorce court only a few years later. All too often this world tells us that love isn't forever, love is just for now. But that is not what God says.

God's love is unconditional.

It is forever.

And it is yours.

God loves you when you get things right, and He loves you when you goof up. He loves you when your life is going great, and He loves you when your life is a mess. He loves you when everything falls into place, and He loves you when everything falls apart. His love never changes.

When we sin, or when life gets hard, it's easy to think that God no longer loves us. Maybe we finally messed up so badly that He has turned His back and abandoned us. People may see us at our worst and run the other way. But not God. When we are at our worst, God runs to us.

You cannot earn God's love, and you cannot lose it. His love is an indisputable fact. Even when you don't feel loved, you are. His love for you is real and unchanging. The circumstances of your life, whether good or bad, are not the measure of how much God loves you. The only measure of His love is the cross.

The apostle John, the only apostle who stood at the foot of the cross and watched Jesus suffer and die, put it this way. "This is love; not that we loved God but that He loved us and sent His Son as an atoning sacrifice for our sins" (1 John 4:10). John saw the measure of God's love as it was poured out on the cross. Jesus Christ bore our sins, our suffering, and our shame. He stood as a shield in front of us and bore the wrath of God in our place. In exchange, He covered us with His righteousness. Every reward, every inheritance, every ounce of His Father's love that belonged to Him, He gave to us while He accepted our punishment. That is how much God loves you.

Feelings will lie to you and circumstances will change, but God's love is unconditional, unchanging, and undeniable. The cross is the eternal evidence of His love for you. You can run from it, you can doubt it, but you cannot lose it. God's love is perfect and it is yours. God loves you, now and forever.

Prayer For Today

MIGHTY GOD,

You are the Father who loves me. You gave Your only Son to save me. Whenever I doubt Your unconditional love for me, remind me of the cross. Thank you for loving me with a perfect, unchanging love. Help me, Lord, to trust the cross when my feelings lie to me. I believe Your words are true. Your love is everlasting. Lord, I love you, too.

Amen

DAY TWO

YOU ARE HEALED

"He himself bore our sins in his body on the cross so that we might die to sin and live for righteousness, by his wounds you have been healed."
1 Peter 2:24

We were crushed under the weight of sin. We were spiritually sick. Then Jesus Christ came into the world, suffered and died on the cross, and brought us healing. We are no longer broken by sin. The blood of Jesus repaired the damage caused by sin and restored us to righteousness; not because of anything we have done, but because of what Jesus did on the cross. By His sacrifice, we have been spiritually healed.

But it doesn't end there. God wants to heal the pain of our past as well. We all have scars and wounds that we carry. Some of them are ones we can see, but many of them are hidden, buried deep, written on our hearts and on our souls. Scars that have built up, creating walls around our hearts. Wounds that linger and pain that seeps out, reminding us of how we've been hurt.

Through the blood of Jesus Christ, we no longer have to carry that pain. He can bring healing to the deepest wounds, the worst memories, and the darkest corners of our heart. There is nothing beyond His reach. His hands are open, waiting for us to surrender the pain of our past and let go of the hurt we have been holding onto. In exchange, He offers us His perfect love and peace.

Letting go can be hard. If we let it go, the people who hurt us might think they're off the hook. We hold on to our pain because we think we deserve to be angry, and we let that anger fester.

But our healing has nothing to do with the person who hurt us and everything to do with the God who loves us. God is willing, right now, to take all the pain that we are holding on to and free us from it. He is ready to embrace us in His love and heal the scars we have carried for so long.

God can be trusted with your pain. He will never make light of it. Scripture says that God captures our tears in a bottle and records our sorrows on His scroll (Psalm 56:8). He has seen your pain, and He wants to heal you from it. Give it to God and walk in the freedom, joy, and peace that He wants for you.

Prayer For Today

MIGHTY GOD,

I know you've seen my pain. You have been with me through it all. You are bigger than anything I've endured. Your love is greater than my hurt. I surrender my past to you. I give you all the scars and wounds that I have held on to. Take them from hands and fill me with your peace. Heal me, Lord, in my body, soul, and spirit. I trust you God, because I know You love me.

Amen

"Yet to all who did receive him, to those who believed in his
name, he gave the right to become children of God."
John 1:12

God is your Creator. He is the Author of life. At His word, you were perfectly formed, knit together in your mother's womb. Every hair on your head was numbered and every day of your life was recorded before your first breath.

God is indeed your Creator, but He is also your Father.

When we accept Jesus Christ as our Savior, when we make Him Lord of our life, we are given the right to become children of God. You are not simply another creation made by the greatest Creator, but His treasured and precious child. You are His family. He is your Father, and He loves you with a Father's love. It is personal, intimate, endless, and unconditional.

As God's child, you have a place in His family. You are a child of God, but you are not childlike. You have been given the rights and privileges of an adult son or daughter. The riches of Heaven are open to you, because your Father makes it available to you. You are not just being tolerated, a black sheep of the family, an outsider trying to sneak into a mansion. You belong in the mansion! It's your Father's house, and it is your eternal home.

The enemy will try to get you to doubt your place in God's family. When he tempted Jesus in the wilderness he taunted him, "*If* you are the Son of God..." He will do the same thing to you. "If," he will say. "If you are God's child."

But God does not lie. His words are true. Galatians 3:26 says, "In Christ Jesus you are all children of God through faith." God has called you His child. He has claimed you as His own. You are His and He loves you with a father's love. If God had a wallet, your photo would be in it.

As His child, you have the right to run to Him. When a child falls and scrapes her knee and runs to her father with tears streaming down her cheeks, she isn't worried about her father's love. She doesn't hesitate or wonder if she will be accepted. That's her father, and she knows that he will sweep her in his arms, comfort her, help her, and love her. That is what you can do. You can run to God, knowing with absolute certainty He will be there to catch you, knowing He is your Father and He loves you.

Prayer For Today

FATHER GOD,

Thank you for loving me as a father loves his child. You call me Your own. Other people may hurt me, but You never will. Your love is unconditional. Help me to remember to run to you when I'm hurting, and to trust that Your love is perfect and unending. When I start to doubt, wrap me in Your love and remind me that I belong to You. You are my Father, and I am your child.

Amen

YOU ARE AN HEIR OF GOD

"Now if we are children, then we are heirs – heirs of God and co-heirs with Christ."
Romans 8:17

*D*oes the word inheritance make you think of a family gathered together in a fancy room while a lawyer reads from someone's will? Does it conjure up images of wills and bequests, of favored children receiving the best, and others receiving nothing? That may be a movie version, but God's view of His heirs is much different.

When we received the gift of salvation in Christ, we became children of God. But we are not only His children, we are also His heirs. This is an important distinction. When Jesus walked the earth, the children and heirs of his time were in different categories. A man could have many children, but only one heir. It was usually the first born who would inherit the father's wealth and standing. The other children would receive much less, if anything, because while they were children, they were not heirs.

God, in His perfect love, flips this. We are His children and also His heirs. Notice in the above Scripture that it says we are heirs and co-heirs with Christ. According to the logic of the world, Jesus Christ as God's first born should be the sole heir. He should inherit everything from His Father, and we should be the ones on the sidelines hoping for a spare coin or two. But that isn't what that verse says. It says not only are we are heirs, but we are co-heirs with Christ. That means we share jointly in His inheritance.

Think about that. Jesus Christ, the heir of Heaven, by His sacrifice has made us co-heirs with Him. Everything God has given Him, Jesus now gives to you. You are not waiting for a left-over inheritance; you will not be forgotten. You are a co-heir with Christ!

An inheritance is not earned, it is given. You cannot earn what God wants to give you. Your place as a co-heir with Christ was secured not by anything you have done or will do. It was given to you by your Father. It is His gift to you as His child. Jesus has withheld nothing from you. He gave his life for you, and now he freely shares his eternal inheritance with you. You are not sneaking into Heaven through a back door, you are walking in as the co-heir of God's riches.

Prayer For Today

HEAVENLY FATHER,
Thank you for choosing me. Thank you making me a part of Your

family. Help me to remember that I am not an afterthought. I am your precious child, a co-heir with Christ. You long to bless me, and Your plan is perfect. No matter what I have or don't have here on Earth, I know there is an inheritance waiting for me in Heaven.

Amen

DAY FIVE

YOU ARE GOD'S MASTERPIECE

"For we are God's handiwork created in Christ Jesus to do good
works which God prepared in advance for us to do."
Ephesians 2:10

*H*ave you ever looked at a beautiful piece of art?
Perhaps a painting or a sculpture that captivated you
and touched your heart, or something so exquisitely crafted you
couldn't help but be in awe of the talent and inspiration that went
into creating it. It is a masterpiece, a work of art created by an
incredible artist. It is *poiema.*

In the Scripture above, the word translated as handiwork
comes from the Greek word *poiema.* In some English transla-
tions, the word used here is workmanship or masterpiece. In the
original Greek, it means something that is crafted or created. It is
where we get the words poem and poetry. It implies the intentional, creative work of a craftsman. A painting made by an artist

is *poiema*. A poem written by a writer is *poiema*. A building designed and constructed by an architect is *poiema*.

You are God's *poiema*.

You have been intentionally and creatively formed by God. He is the artist, and you are His masterpiece. God has taken all the raw materials of your past, present, and future, all of your gifts and talents, every quirk of your personality, every cell of your body, and created a masterpiece. As magnificent as the snow-covered mountains or a sunset over the ocean, as awe-inspiring as the brightest star, and as unique as each winter snow, you are an extraordinary work of art. You are not an accident.

Can I say that again? You are not an accident. You were created by The Divine Artist. Just as a painter carefully considers his palette, as a sculptor examines the stone, as a poet ponders her every word, God formed you with care, consideration, and purpose. You are His workmanship, His work of art, His master-piece. You are a poem written by the Author of the universe.

Where we were once marred by sin, smudged and broken, the blood of Jesus has restored us to the original beauty God created us to be. We are not perfect, and we never will be, but the One who created us is, and He created us to be His.

When the world wants to tear you down and remind you of your failings, when insecurity raises its nasty head, and doubt tries to surface, remind yourself that you are a work of art. You are God's masterpiece.

Prayer For Today

MIGHTY GOD,

Thank you for creating me. Thank you for making me Your work of art. Thank you for taking the broken pieces of my life and making me a masterpiece. Help me to remember today and every day that I am Yours, and that You have made me beautiful.

Amen

DAY SIX

YOU ARE NEVER ALONE

"Never will I leave you; never will I forsake you."
Hebrews 13:5

*L*oneliness is a terrible feeling. To feel alone in our struggles, to be misunderstood, left to our own devices, or abandoned when we need help the most is a hollow, exhausting, and discouraging feeling.

And you never have to feel it again.

When you accept Jesus Christ as your Savior, you have taken your last step on your own. From that moment on you have a friend, a Father, a comforter, a defender, a protector, a family, and a home. You will never be alone again. No matter where you go, what you do, how you struggle, or when you fail, God will never leave you. You are His, and He will walk with you, day by day, step by step, every mile of the journey until He welcomes you into eternity.

In this verse from Hebrews, God says that He will never leave you or forsake you. In the original Greek language, leave and forsake are two different words and they mean different things. There are two distinct promises from God in this one verse.

The first promise is God will not leave you. This word is also translated at times as fail. God will not fail you. In the original language, this word means that God will not slacken, cease, or give up on you. God is fighting for you and He will never give up on you. You are never a lost cause to Him. God is on your side and He will not fail.

The second promise is God will not forsake you. The word used here means to desert, abandon, leave destitute, or leave helpless. Imagine being in a battle and your partner runs away leaving you to face the enemy on your own. That is what it means to be forsaken, to be left to fight, struggle, and suffer on your own.

God will not forsake you. He will never turn away and leave you on your own. He will not leave you when things get bad, and He will not desert you when you fall.

God has promised to never leave you or forsake you. He will never give up on you and He will never abandon you. God will remain by your side, in success and failure, on the highest mountain, and in the deepest pit. He will never stop fighting for you, and He will never leave you to face your battles alone.

Prayer For Today

MIGHTY GOD,

Thank you for being my constant companion. Thank you for

walking with me, for staying beside me, and fighting for me. Your word says You will never leave me or forsake me. Whatever comes, I know You will be with me. You are my constant companion. I do not have to face my days on my own because You are with me.

Amen

"I no longer call you servants because a servant does not know his master's business. Instead I have called you friends, for everything that I learned from my Father I have made known to you."
John 15:15

There are two very different ways to approach God: as His servant or as His friend. Do we serve God? Yes. Is it right to serve Him, our church, and our family? Absolutely. But are we only servants? No. We are His friends.

Imagine being at a wedding in the time of Jesus. The bride and groom invite their family and closest friends to share in their celebration. Friends surround the happy couple, sharing in their joy, and wishing them well. Servants drift in and out of the rooms bringing food and drink, making sure the celebration runs smoothly. Friends are invited guests. Servants are not. Friends are there out of love; servants are there out of duty.

Jesus does not call us servants. He calls us friends. He has brought us into his confidence. He has built a relationship with us. The word used for friend in the original Greek implies intimacy, close friendship, and companionship. It is the word used to describe those who attended the bridegroom at his wedding, a word used to describe the men asked by the groom to stand beside him. It is the same word used to describe Abraham as a friend of God. Jesus used this same word to describe Lazarus as his friend.

We have been brought into close fellowship with God. We are not servants forced to attend Him. We are honored friends chosen to be by His side.

Friends are the people you can call to celebrate good news with and console you in bad news. Friends know us and understand us. They love us with all of our faults and failings and enjoy spending time with us. That is what God desires to have with us. He wants to be our close friend.

The more time we spend with God by praying, reading His Word, and worshipping Him, the closer we will be to Him. Friendships are not formed by accident, they are built on relationship. They are cultivated, nurtured, and developed. If you want a closer friendship with God, spend time with Him. Talk to Him. God is ready to be the best friend you could ever have.

Prayer For Today

Dear God,

Thank you for being my friend. When I am lonely, help me remember that I am never alone. You are always by my side, a best friend who will never leave me. Thank you for reaching out to me even when I didn't deserve it. Teach me how to be closer to You, to spend time with You, and to know You more.

Amen

DAY EIGHT

YOU ARE NO LONGER A SLAVE TO SIN

"For we know that our old self was crucified with him so that the old body ruled by sin might be done away with, that we should no longer be slaves to sin."
Romans 6:6

I heard a story once about a young woman who lived in a communist country. Though she was famous around the world, she was a prisoner of the state, forced to wear a smile in public while suffering in the shadows. Her freedom was taken away, her family was threatened, and her life was in danger. She was a slave to the government of her country, until the day she made a daring escape and defected. She renounced her citizenship in the communist nation and embraced the citizenship of the country that had given her sanctuary. She was no longer a slave to one country because she lived in freedom in another.

That is the picture God is painting in this verse. We were slaves to the nation of sin. We were prisoners, unable to break free from the chains that bound us. We were in the hands of the enemy. Our citizenship was in sin.

But when Jesus bore the punishment for our sins on the cross, the prison door was opened and we were set free. When we accepted the gift of salvation we defected. Our chains were broken. We evaded the enemy who held us captive and ran to a new nation while God Himself held open the door for us. "For he has rescued us from the dominion of darkness and brought us into the kingdom of the Son he loves" (Colossians 1:13). Freedom is available to us in God's kingdom. Our citizenship is now in Heaven.

Because you are no longer a slave to sin, Satan has no power to command or control you. He has no right to you because you belong to God. You don't have to give in to the temptations of sin because you are a citizen of a new land. Satan can whisper to us: he can try to convince us that we aren't worthy, that we don't deserve the gift that has been given to us. He will try to draw us back to the land we escaped, to call us back to the country of sin and darkness by telling us that we belong there.

But he is wrong, and he is a liar. Your citizenship is eternal. You belong to God's kingdom, set free from the chains of your past and prepared for the blessing and goodness God has prepared for you.

Prayer For Today

MIGHTY GOD,

Thank you for rescuing me from a life of sin and darkness and welcoming me into Your kingdom. I am no longer a slave to sin, but I am Your friend and Your child. Strengthen me to stand firm in the freedom and blessings You have given me and to not look back. I belong to You and no one can take me from Your hand.

Amen

YOU ARE A NEW CREATION

"Therefore, if anyone is in Christ, the new creation has come:
The old is gone, the new is here."
2 Corinthians 5:17

You are not your past.

We have all made mistakes. We've made poor choices; we've gone down wrong roads. We've done things that we aren't proud of, and some of those decisions have followed us for years, defining us, and labeling us. Addict. Failure. Cheater. Wild. Reckless. The list goes on and on, and there are plenty of people who love to remind us of those labels, and tell us over and over how badly we messed up. And sometimes, we don't need anyone else to remind us of our past, we do it enough on our own. Our minds play our mistakes on a loop that runs through our head, regrets that pile up, steal our sleep, and cause us to doubt our future.

That is not God.

Jesus comes and makes all things new. When you lifted your eyes to the cross and opened your heart to Jesus Christ, you were changed. Transformed. Made new. Your past no longer defines you. God does.

God knows who you are. He knows everything about you. He knows every detail of your past. He knows every mistake, every regret, every missed opportunity, and He still calls you a new creation.

Why? Because when Jesus shed His blood for you, He wiped away your past. He took it all and gave you a clean slate. He covered you with His righteousness and gave you the right to stand before God without condemnation, fear, or regret. God didn't cover you with a fresh coat of paint to hide your mistakes. He made you something entirely new.

Your past doesn't define you. It defines God. It defines His redemptive power. Your past is not a badge of shame for you to wear; it is a badge of honor for God to wear. The mistakes of your past, the disappointments, hurts, and regrets have become victory banners that proclaim God's love, grace, and mercy. Your past cannot define you because you are a new creation, formed perfectly by the hands of the God who loves you.

Prayer For Today

FATHER GOD,

Thank you for redeeming my past. You have raised me up out of the disappointments and mistakes I've made and given me a fresh start. I am a new creation, formed by Your hand and set free to walk in right-

eousness and holiness. When the labels of my past try to define me, give me strength to turn away and remember that You have made me new. I am who You say I am, and You say I am Yours.

Amen

DAY TEN

YOU ARE FREE

"You will know the truth, and the truth will set you free."
John 8:32

Does your faith ever feel like an obligation? A list of things to do? Read the Bible…check. Pray…check. Go to church…check. Do you ever worry that you're not doing enough? That God might be mad at you because you aren't a "perfect" Christian? If that's you, then this will be good news.

You are enough.

God doesn't want you to check the boxes of your faith, He wants your heart. The world may tell us that we have to earn God's love, but God tells us that His love is a gift.

The world may tell us we have to be perfect for God to love us, but God says He loved us when we were still lost sinners.

The world may tell us that we have to work hard to keep God's love, but God says that nothing can separate us from His love.

God isn't setting you up for failure. He didn't welcome you into His family only to kick you out again if you mess up. His grace is free and so is His love. You cannot earn what he has already given you. You cannot lose what He has promised. Too often we embrace the free gift of salvation only to sink into legalism once we're there. Duty replaces love, obligation replaces delight. Worry replaces joy. We think we have to do more and be more to convince God over and over that we are worthy of His attention.

And nothing could be further from the truth. The grace you received at salvation is the same grace God offers to you now. He doesn't want your duty, He wants your heart. When you stop checking boxes and start delighting in the Lord, you have freedom to fellowship. You are free to be who God created you to be. You are free to worship Him without fear. You are free to call Him Father. You are free to embrace the Holy Spirit and develop the gifts He has given you. You are free to trust that God's love is unconditional and His grace is eternal.

Prayer For Today

DEAR LORD,

Thank you for setting me free from obligation. Help me worship You because I love You, not because I have to. I know You accomplished everything on the cross and there is nothing I can do to earn the love You have already given me. I want to walk in the freedom that Your love and grace gives me, free to be who You created me to be and to love You with my whole heart.

Amen

DAY ELEVEN

YOU ARE FORGIVEN

"In him we have redemption through his blood, the forgiveness
of sins, in accordance with the riches of God's grace."
Ephesians 1:7

When we were having construction work done on our backyard, bills started rolling in. The concrete supplier had an invoice. The rain gutter installer had a bill of sale. The landscaper had a list of services he'd completed. Bills. Invoices. Debts. We had incurred a list of charges that we needed to pay for. It was our choice to have the work done and it was our responsibility to pay our debts.

Before we accepted Jesus into our lives, we had a spiritual debt to pay. We sinned over and over again and eventually that bill would have to be paid. The bad news is there is no way to pay our debt to God. He is holy, perfect, and sinless. There is nothing we can offer and nothing we can do to pay the debt of our sin. No amount of good works can ever cover the cost.

But the Gospel is good news. Jesus Christ stepped forward to pay the debt for us. Through His sacrifice on the cross, His blood paid our debt. When Jesus died on the cross, our debt wasn't just marked "Paid in Full," it was erased. The debt we owed was forgiven.

To forgive a debt is to wipe it out, to cancel it, to lay it aside. Because of the sacrifice of Jesus Christ, God keeps no record of your wrongs. Jesus didn't place a check mark in your ledger, He took your ledger away. He put his name on it, assuming all of your sin and all of your debt. In exchange, He gave you a ledger that is completely clean.

This great exchange is an act of grace and mercy. We don't deserve it; we didn't earn it; we didn't negotiate it; we can certainly never pay it back. It was an act of will, an intentional choice by God because of His unending and unconditional love for you. The final words Jesus spoke on the cross were, "It is finished." (John 19:30). In the original Greek, this phrase is *tetelestai* which means complete. Jesus Christ's work on the cross is complete. It is finished. His sacrifice is eternal. The debt of your sin was forgiven forever by His death. You can stand before God without fear of condemnation or punishment because there is literally nothing to condemn. Your record is clean because of the cross.

Prayer For Today

FATHER GOD,

Thank you for the cross. Thank you for the sacrifice of Your Son to make me clean. I receive the free gift of His salvation and I praise You for it. I know that when you look at me you don't see the record of my wrongs. Help me always remember how much I have been forgiven, so I can extend that forgiveness to others.

Amen

DAY TWELVE

YOU ARE REDEEMED

"I have swept away your offenses like a cloud, your sins like the
morning mist. Return to me for I have redeemed you."
Isaiah 44:22

t first glance, the words forgiven and redeemed look a
lot alike. Many times, we use these words interchange-
ably without thinking too much about it, but these are two
different words. When Jesus died on the cross, our sins were
forgiven. They were set aside and cast as far as the east is from
the west (Psalm 103:12). But the forgiveness of sins wasn't the
only work accomplished on the cross. The death of Jesus also
redeemed us.

The word redemption is often applied to the idea of buying a
slave's freedom. When someone was sold into slavery, they could
be redeemed for a price. That price would buy the slave's freedom. A slave could save up enough money to redeem himself and

buy his own freedom, or someone else could redeem him. By paying the ransom price, the redeemer secured a slave's freedom.

We were the slaves. We were in bondage to sin and death, chained to our past and destined for destruction. Then Jesus came and paid the ransom to redeem us. He gave up his life on the cross to buy us back from the kingdom of darkness.

At the dawn of creation, we belonged to God. Humanity walked with Him in a paradise, perfectly in harmony with Him and creation. Then disobedience entered the garden, and we lost that fellowship. We became slaves to sin. Through the cross, Jesus bought us back. He ransomed us and paid the price to set us free.

Think of the things you spend a great deal of money to buy: your house, your car, expensive technology, or jewelry. The things you invest a lot of money in become the things you hold most dear. They are valuable because you paid a hefty price for them.

Now think of the price God paid for you. He didn't buy you with gold, silver, or money. He paid for you with the life of His only Son. How valuable you are to God! He loved you so much He paid an unimaginable price, He gave everything for you. You were redeemed by the life of Jesus Christ. Your freedom was purchased through His blood and you belong to Him. You are His treasured possession.

Prayer For Today

HOLY FATHER,

You are my God, and I am Yours. Jesus purchased my life with His blood and set me free to live the life You have planned for me. Help me remember that You love me so much that You gave Your only Son for me. Let me walk each day knowing that I am your treasured child.

    Amen

YOU ARE SEALED WITH THE HOLY SPIRIT

"When you believed you were marked in him with a seal, the
promised Holy Spirit."
Ephesians 1:13

When we studied the Middle Ages in our homeschooling, my children were fascinated with seals and signet rings. We used candle wax to practice setting seals on letters. They put wax seals on every scrap of paper they could find, and they never got the papers mixed up because the seal showed who it belonged to.

A seal is a symbol of authority and protection. When Daniel was thrown into the lions' den, the king sealed the entrance to the den. No one could break the seal of the king. When Jesus was buried, Pilate ordered the tomb to be sealed with his signet.

The seal was also a sign of ownership. It showed possession and if a dispute arose, it was evidence that would point to the rightful owner.

When you believed in Jesus Christ as your Savior, you were sealed with the Holy Spirit. That seal rests on you as a sign of God's authority, protection, and ownership. It is as if you have been stamped with the signet ring of God. His seal is on you, and it tells the world and every power of Hell that you belong to Him. God is the author of your life. Your steps are ordered by Him. Your life is sealed with His Name.

You are filled and sealed with the Holy Spirit and that gives you authority in the Name of God. You have His authority to speak life where there is darkness, to proclaim truth where there are lies, and to speak healing where there is brokenness.

The seal of the Holy Spirit is also a mark of protection over you. God will never leave you or forsake you. His protection rests on you. In this life, you will face trials and hard times, but His divine protection will be with you to help and sustain you.

This seal marks you as God's treasured possession. You belong to Him. No effort of the world, and no scheme of Satan can take you from His hand. He has set His seal upon you and claimed you for His kingdom. You are not alone in the battle, you are not adrift on the seas. You belong to the King of Heaven, and His seal is unbreakable.

Prayer For Today

MIGHTY GOD,

Thank you for picking me out of the mess of my past and setting Your seal upon me. You are the Author of my life, and You have brought me into the light of Your presence. No matter what comes, I know that I belong to You. Your Holy Spirit is within me. Help me walk in the authority You have given me and trust in Your protection every day of my life.

    Amen

"But our citizenship is in Heaven."
Philippians 3:20

I love to travel. I'm an expert at living out of a carry-on bag and packing the perfect snacks (and books) for a long flight. But one thing I am never fully prepared for is the long lines when entering a foreign country. Waiting to present my passport and enter a new country can be a time-consuming process. There are questions and an inspection of my documents, all done to verify that I will be allowed in. It's always a relief when I return from a trip and go through the line for US residents, knowing this is my home.

As Christians, our citizenship is in Heaven. We live in this world, but we are citizens of another. When we die, we will have no fear of not being allowed into Heaven because our spiritual passports are already in order. This world is not our home. Our home is in Heaven, and our citizenship has been secured by the blood of Jesus Christ. While we work, live, laugh, and love in this world, one day we will return to our eternal home. There will be no waiting in line, no doubt or fear, because our name is already written in His book.

When I travel, my identity is as an American. I represent my country, for good or for ill, as I visit new places. I am an unofficial ambassador for the United States. People may judge my country by my actions and my words. As citizens of Heaven we are ambassadors for God. "We are therefore Christ's ambassadors as though God were making His appeal through us" (2 Corinthians 5:20). We bear the name of Christ to this world. We are His representatives on earth; His hands, His feet, His voice to those around us. You may not be a preacher, a Bible teacher, or a missionary, but you are still a representative of Heaven. You have been entrusted with the message of the Gospel and it is yours to share.

No matter where we go or what we do, as citizens of Heaven, God is our sovereign. Presidents, kings, senators, and dictators come and go, but our King is eternal. Nothing that happens on earth can shake Heaven. God is on the throne, our King and our Lord, and He is in control. Our citizenship is in a land that will never perish. We are visiting this world, passing through until we are called home to the place God has prepared for us.

Prayer For Today

LORD,

Thank you for being the King of my life. You have given me a home in Heaven, and You are already preparing a place for me for eternity. When life in this world gets hard, remind me that my home is with You. Help me represent You with boldness and love, compassion and wisdom in a world that needs You now more than ever.

   Amen

DAY FIFTEEN

YOU ARE CHOSEN

"For we know brothers and sisters loved by God, that He has
chosen you."
1 Thessalonians 1:4

*D*o you remember choosing teams in elementary school? The teacher would line up all the students and select team captains. The captains would then take turns choosing people for their teams. No one wanted to be chosen last. It didn't matter how fun the game was or whether your team won or lost, that sinking feeling of being the last one chosen stung. All these years later, it might still sting.

But here's some good news, in God's timeline you are not the last one chosen. Not even close. The Bible says God chose you before He formed the world (Ephesians 1:4). Before the world was created, before your great-great-great grandparents were even born, God knew you and He chose you to be His. He wasn't choosing you for a kickball team, He chose you for His family. He chose you to be His child. He chose you to be His partner in the work He set aside for you to do.

Back in recess, some kids were picked first because they had athletic talent. Some might have been picked first because they were popular or because their best friend was the team captain. But that is not how God works. You don't have to prove yourself to God because He chose you before you were born. You don't have to earn your way onto His team or show off your skills because the choosing has already been done. God chose you because He loves you.

"You did not choose me, but I chose you and appointed you that you should go and bear fruit - fruit that will last" (John 15:16).

You are not a last pick. You are not an after-thought. God is not stuck with you. You are not sneaking into Heaven through some loophole. You were hand selected by God. You are wanted. You are valuable. God knew you before you knew yourself, and He chose you. God chose you before you were born because He saw you, and He loved you.

Prayer For Today

FATHER GOD,

Thank you for choosing me. You formed me, created me and chose me before I was even born. You set me aside as Your chosen child. You called me and anointed me. When I feel discouraged or let down by others, help me remember that Your love is eternal, and that You have chosen me to belong to You. You have called me out of darkness and into the light of Your presence.

Amen

DAY SIXTEEN

YOU ARE KNOWN

"But whoever loves God is known by God."
1 Corinthians 8:3

In my early years as a Christian, I had the feeling that I was being swept along with the crowd of people going to Heaven. I thought I was just one in a billion--a faceless, nameless human sneaking my way into Heaven. I knew God, but I highly doubted He knew me. How could He possibly know tiny, insignificant me when He had the whole universe to worry about?

It took years of growing in my faith and sitting under loving pastors and mentors for me to understand that God not only knows my name, He knows the number of hairs on my head! He knows the number of hairs on your head, too. God knows you… you personally. The prophet Jeremiah put it this way, "Yet, You know me, Lord; You see me" (Jeremiah 12:3). You are personally, intimately, and deeply known by God.

God is the God of the universe, but He is also your God. It is a personal relationship. You are not a number to Him, not one more person in the crowd. He sees you, and He knows you.

God knows your name and He knows your heart. He has seen every day of your life. He knows your most cherished memory and your deepest disappointment. He knows your most painful regret and your secret ambition. He knows your every hope, dream, fear, and worry. He saw the betrayal that broke your heart, and the loss that brought you to your knees. He knows your greatest success and your hidden sin. God knows it all.

And He loves you.

Nothing can separate you from His love. There is no need to walk on eggshells around God, afraid of Him discovering what you want to hide. He already knows it. There is no need to sugar-coat your prayers, cover up your ambition, or bury your dreams; He knows those, too. Nothing is hidden from God. He created you, and He knows you. There's no need to pretend, to fake your way through, or try to be something you're not. God can't be fooled, so there's no need to try. When you come before God, you can be exactly who you are. You can pour out your heart to Him and trust that He will not turn away. God knows you and He loves you, just as you are.

Prayer For Today

MIGHTY GOD,

Thank you for standing beside me no matter what. You know every secret in my heart. You have caught all my tears and seen my every pain. You know everything about me and You love me. I can be myself with You and trust You with the deepest desires of my heart. Thank you for seeing me and for knowing me.

Amen

YOU ARE FEARFULLY AND WONDERFULLY MADE

"I praise You because I am fearfully and wonderfully made."
Psalm 139:14

You are not an accident. You are not the result of cosmic coincidence, random chance, or dumb luck. You are carefully, thoughtfully, and intentionally created by God. No matter the circumstances of your birth, you were created by God with purpose and for a reason.

When so much of the world seems to be spinning out of control, when so much seems uncertain, when random acts of violence swirl around us, it can be hard to believe there is purpose behind it all. Even our lives can seem to be tossed about on the winds of chance and circumstance.

But your life is not a random event. God has a plan and a purpose for you. He had a plan for you before He laid the foundations of the world. He knew the right time and the right place for your birth. He chose this time and this place for you to live out your calling. Circumstances cannot surprise God. He isn't caught off guard. And He doesn't make mistakes. He knew exactly what He was doing when He formed you. He knit you together in your mother's womb, designing you, filling you with His gifts, and equipping you for this world.

One of my favorite Scriptures comes from the book of Esther. A young Jewish girl who was unexpectedly raised to royalty is confronted with a choice: risk her life to save her people from annihilation, or remain silent and try to save her own life. As she considers her options, her uncle tells her, "And who knows but that you have to come to your royal position for such a time as this" (Esther 4:14).

You are royalty, an heir to the King of Heaven. You have come to this royal position for such as time as this. This world. This time. This city. This school. This job. This family. God knew exactly what He was doing.

An artist doesn't slap together a work of art. A writer doesn't randomly choose words. Each brushstroke, each word is a choice. God was intentional when he created you. Even with your weaknesses and the things you don't like or wish you could change, you are fearfully and wonderfully made, intentionally and deliberately designed. You were purposefully and joyfully created for such a time as this.

Prayer For Today

HEAVENLY FATHER,

Thank you for creating me. I believe there is a purpose for my life, and I believe that You have created me for such a time as this. I offer You all I have. Lead me in the direction of Your sending and equip me to do Your will in this world. Where You lead, I will follow.

Amen

DAY EIGHTEEN

YOU ARE ABLE

"I can do all things through Christ who gives me strength."
Philippians 4:13 (NKJV)

This verse is much more than a motivational saying. We may like to quote it to encourage someone, or talk ourselves into trying something scary, but that misses the point. This verse isn't about being daring or giving yourself a pep talk. It's far better.

This verse is about endurance. When the apostle Paul wrote this letter to the church at Philippi, he had been stoned, flogged, shipwrecked, tortured, and imprisoned. He had been hungry, persecuted, and mocked. He had also seen the power of God move in the hearts of new believers, and he'd seen countless people come to salvation. He had witnessed the move of God in his own life and in the lives of those he pastored. Paul had experienced incredible highs and heartbreaking lows, and he learned that he could endure it all, the good and the bad, the greatest victories and the harshest defeats, because of the strength Christ gives.

You can endure anything because of Jesus Christ. The changing circumstances of life cannot overwhelm you, trample you, or destroy you because Jesus Christ is your strength. And His strength is enough.

That is much better than a pep talk.

God has not promised us a trouble-free, successful-filled existence. Quite the opposite, in fact. He tells us that we will have trouble. We will face hardship. Things will go wrong. But He also tells us that He will be with us when it happens. We will be able to endure because of Jesus.

This verse is a message of hope. It's about remembering our dependency on Jesus, and His promise to be with us. You are able to withstand the storms of life. You will not be defeated by a diagnosis, bad news, or hardship. You will not be overwhelmed by the hatred of others, the disappointments or discouragements of life because you have the strength of Jesus Christ. Because of His strength you are able to stand, to rise up, to take one more step. You are able to be content and live in peace, unshaken by whatever comes at you because the strength that lives in you comes from God, and it cannot be broken.

Prayer For Today

DEAR LORD,

Strengthen me when I'm weak. Encourage me when I worry. Lift me up when I fall down. I need You, Lord. Fill me afresh with the strength that comes from You. Help me look above my circumstances and keep my eyes focused on You. I can endure all things with You by my side. Thank you for never leaving me.

Amen

"In all these things we are more than conquerors through him
who loved us."
Romans 8:37

The phrase "more than conquerors" in this verse is one word in the original Greek. The word is *hupernikao*. It is actually two words smashed into one to convey a particular thought. The word *huper* means over and the word *nikao* means victory. Put them together and you get *hupernikao*. So, the phrase could be translated as overwhelmingly victorious. It isn't just a victory, it's a decisive victory, a "completely-demolished-the-other-guy" type of victory. It's the like a 150-0 final score in a football game. The losing team was outmatched and utterly destroyed.

In the spiritual battle we face, it is Satan who is against us. He is the enemy of our souls, and he has been defeated. The cross was an overwhelming victory. When Jesus declared in John 19:30, "It is finished," that wasn't a word of defeat but of victory. The war was over, and it was an overwhelming victory.

You can walk in confidence because you're on the winning side. The battle has been won. God is the victor. His promises are true and eternal. Nothing can steal us away from His hand because the enemy has been defeated. Jesus conquered sin and death and opened the gates of Heaven. We have no fear of death because of what Jesus accomplished. Your future is secure. Your reward is waiting for you. You can walk with the boldness of a conquering soldier because your commander won the battle before you even picked up your weapon.

You have the right to share in the victory of Jesus Christ because He won it for you. You were the prize. You were what He was fighting for. Satan will fight, manipulate, tempt, and try to steal you from God's hand, but he won't succeed unless you allow it. A defeated enemy has no right to what the victor has won. His hold on you has been broken by the cross.

The next two verses say, "For I am convinced that neither death nor life, neither angels nor demons, neither the present nor the future, nor any powers, neither height nor depth, nor anything else in all creation, will be able to separate us from the love of God that is in Christ Jesus our Lord" (Romans 8:38-39). Nothing can separate you from God and the victory He has won.

Prayer For Today

MIGHTY GOD,

You are a mighty warrior, a conqueror who has defeated Hell, death, and the grave. Satan cannot stand against you. He is a defeated enemy. You won the victory on the cross, so I will walk in boldness and confidence knowing that nothing can snatch me from Your hand. I am victorious because of Your love.

    Amen

DAY TWENTY

YOU ARE AN OVERCOMER

"And they overcame him by the blood of the Lamb and by the
word of their testimony."
Revelation 12:11 (NKJV)

Through Jesus Christ we are more than conquerors.
Victory is ours, but we are fighting a battle against an
enemy who doesn't want to admit defeat. Our reward is secure,
our eternity has been decided, but the battle still rages. Conflict
will happen, trouble will come, but you have everything you need
to overcome those battles. You are an overcomer.

This verse from Revelation gives us the weapons we need to
overcome the attacks of Satan: the blood of Jesus and the word of
our testimony.

It is through the shed blood of Jesus Christ that the victory
has been won. This weapon always comes first because without
Jesus, nothing else will work. Our strength, our confidence, and

our authority all flow from Him. He goes before us and makes a way. We can overcome the attacks of the enemy because we know the battle is already won.

In the Old Testament the Israelites often set up memorial stones to stand as testimonies to what God had done. When they saw those stones, they would remember His miracles. They told those stories to their children. The stones stood as witnesses to what God had done for them.

The word of our testimony is a memorial stone in our life. When we remember and share our testimony we are speaking the truth of God's presence, love, and grace. We are raising a standard against the enemy, proclaiming the power of God to a world that needs to hear it. These words are a reminder of what God has done for us.

Our testimony can be an encouragement to others as well. When we share what God has done for us, we can inspire others to lift their eyes to Him, open their hearts, and hold on to faith. Sharing what God has done in our life can bring healing and blessing in the lives of others. Your testimony is a memorial stone that others will see. When they ask, "What does this mean?" you can tell them the story of the God who loves us and who gave His Son for us. Your testimony is a weapon to overcome, to stand firm, and to proclaim the victory of God.

Prayer For Today

DEAR LORD,

You have worked miracles in my life. Nothing is greater than the miracle of salvation. You rescued me from darkness and brought me into the light of Your love and grace. It was Your power that set me free. Help me share what You have done for me. Give me words to speak that glorify Your name and tell others about Your love.

    Amen

YOU ARE THE LIGHT OF THE WORLD

"You are the light of the world."
Matthew 5:14

When Jesus ascended to Heaven after His resurrection, He promised to send the Holy Spirit to believers, and He kept His promise. The Holy Spirit dwells within us, living inside each and every one of us. God doesn't just walk before us, beside us, and behind us, He is within us in the power and presence of the Holy Spirit. We have been filled with the light Jesus brought into the world, and because it now lives within us, Jesus has declared that we are the light of the world.

In a world full of darkness and corruption, you are light. It is the light of God that shines through you. You have been given a precious treasure. You know the secret to life, peace, and victory. Eternity is open before you because of your faith in Jesus Christ.

You have the light that chases away the darkness, and you can share that with the world.

Imagine a dark room. Pitch black. No way to find the door and only darkness and shadows everywhere. Now imagine a single candle flaring to life, a single flame in the midst of the darkness. The light of that candle will dispel the darkness because darkness cannot exist in the presence of light.

Jesus has filled you with His light. Your life is a light that shines in a fallen world. Your words, your life, and your actions reflect the light of Jesus Christ. Our light shines, not to point to us, but to point to God. We shine so that others will see Him. It is God's light shining through us that makes the darkness flee.

Light is not meant to be hidden. No one turns on a light and then smothers it. We turn on a light to see, to find our way. The light of Christ within you is the same. It isn't there to be hidden. It's there to shine, to show the way through the darkness. Your faith is meant to shine. Set your light on the highest hill you can find and shine brightly. Remember, a lighthouse shines brightest in the darkest storm. Stand firm in your faith and let your light shine.

Prayer For Today

FATHER GOD,

You sent Your Son into the world to be a light in the darkness. You have filled me with Your Holy Spirit and given me a light to carry. Help me shine brightly. Let my light be a beacon that shows others the way to You. I will not give in to fear or anxiety, but I will trust You to show me how to shine the brightest.

Amen

"And you are complete in Him."
Colossians 2:10 (NKJV)

Turn on the television, scroll through social media, flip through a magazine and you will find plenty of people telling you that you aren't enough, or that your life is missing something. Usually they will offer to provide you with whatever it is they say you're missing…for a hefty price. Modern culture has turned making us feel insecure, unworthy, and incomplete into a multi-billion-dollar-a-year industry.

But here's the truth, you are enough. Right now. This minute. You are enough. God loves you just as you are and there is nothing you have to do to earn, keep, or increase His love for you. He has filled you with His Holy Spirit and given you everything you need to be exactly who He created you to be.

As human beings, we tend to focus on our imperfections and

the things we lack. We would like to be taller, shorter, thinner, fitter, smarter, or more talented. We think we need more money, more skills, a better job, or a nicer car. We have a long list of things we would like to change about ourselves. If only I had this one thing, then I would have it all. If only I looked this way, then I would be happy. But nothing the world offers can fill our hearts. We are searching for a completeness we can only find in God, and there isn't a person anywhere on earth who can fill His shoes. This world, and everything in it, is passing away. We have been called to eternity in the presence of God and nothing temporary can satisfy that yearning.

The good news is that you already have all of God. He has held nothing back from you. God does not portion out His love or His presence to you. He doesn't pass it out bit by bit, keeping some in reserve just in case He changes His mind. He gave it all to you. The fullness of His grace was poured out on you the moment you accepted Jesus Christ as your Savior. He has withheld nothing from you.

There is unspeakable joy waiting for us in Heaven. No more tears, no more pain, and no more death. We will be in the presence of God forever. That is something to look forward to, a miracle that we will one day experience. But as we wait, here and now, you are worthy, you are whole, you have all of God. You are complete in Christ.

Prayer For Today

FATHER GOD,
Thank you for making me whole. You rescued me and filled me with

Your love and grace. Help me remember that I lack nothing. You are all I will ever need and You have already given me the fullness of Your presence. I am complete in You.

Amen

"We have different gifts, according to the grace given to each
of us."
Romans 12:6

I have always wanted to be a painter. I can spend hours wandering through museums, staring at the works of art that line the walls. Looking at the beautiful paintings created by incredibly talented artists, I yearn to pick up a brush and paint, to make something beautiful. Unfortunately, I have no talent for painting. None. Even stick figures are beyond my artistic capabilities. I don't have a gift for that kind of art, but I know God has given me other gifts.

And He's given you gifts as well. God has blessed you with gifts that He chose specifically for you. He has filled you, equipped you, and anointed you with gifts that are perfectly suited to the purpose He has for you. Maybe you're a writer, a painter, or a singer. Maybe you have a gift for prayer or encouragement. Maybe you have been blessed with gifts for leadership, organization, accounting, or math. The gifts of God are boundless and limitless. They are His gifts to give as He chooses, and He has given you exactly what you need to fulfill His purpose for your life.

I used to be jealous of people who paint and draw. Then I realized that I didn't need to be jealous of someone else's gift, because I have my own. God has blessed me just as much as He has blessed the artists I admire. He has done the same for you. Your gifts are different, but they're yours, and that makes them special.

There is no point in being jealous of what we don't have or wishing for the one thing we don't possess when we have something much better already in our hands. We have gifts perfectly chosen for us by God. We cannot walk in the power and purpose God has for us if we keep trying to use someone else's gift. The power of God in our life flows when we embrace the gifts He has given us.

Prayer For Today

FATHER GOD,

Thank you for filling me with Your Holy Spirit. I receive the gifts You have given me. Help me to use those gifts to glorify You. Show me what they are, teach me how to develop them, and bring me opportunities to use them. I trust that You have a plan and a purpose for me, and that You have given me everything I need to walk in it.

Amen

YOU ARE NOT FORGOTTEN

"Can a woman forget the baby at her breast, and have no compassion on the child she has borne? Though she may forget, I will not forget you! See I have engraved you on the palms of my hands."
Isaiah 49:15-16

When life is hard, when it feels like no one is listening to our prayers, when the answers we so desperately seek don't come, it can be easy to think that God has forgotten us. We feel alone, unheard, and forgotten.

But God has promised that He will never forget you. This verse says that a mother would forget her own child before God could forget you. You are engraved on the palms of His hands. When Jesus appeared to the disciples after His resurrection, He showed them the scars on His hands and feet and the wound in His side. Jesus carries the only scars in Heaven, and He carries them for us. God cannot forget you because you are written on the palms of His hands.

We may feel forgotten, but we are not forgotten. That is an important distinction. We may go through times of sorrow and pain, loneliness and disappointment. People may let us down, it may even feel like God has let us down, but feelings are not truth. Feelings change, God's promises do not.

God does not forget us, but sometimes we forget God. We forget that He is faithful. We forget that He keeps His promises. We forget that He is in control. We forget that His love is unconditional, boundless, and never ending. The circumstances of life may try to tell us that God is taking too long, that He isn't listening, or that He has forgotten His promise to us. Those are lies. God has engraved us on His palms, our names put there by the nails that were driven through His hands on the cross.

You are not forgotten. God is with you. He hears your prayers. He bottles your tears. He walks beside you in every storm. You are His and He remembers His promises. When discouragement rises, when anxiety builds, or when whispers of doubt begin, remember who God is. He is your Father, your Savior and your Comforter. He has not forgotten you and He is at work even when you can't feel it. Hold tight to His promises and remember God is with you.

Prayer For Today

MIGHTY GOD,

I believe that You are with me. Even when I can't feel it, I trust that You are here. You are beside me and You have never left me. You will never forget me because I am engraved on the palms of Your hands. Help me remember who You are and hold onto Your promises and Your Word. What You say is true, and You have promised to never forget me.

Amen

"And my God will meet all your needs according to the riches of
His glory in Christ Jesus."
Philippians 4:19

Have you ever looked at the story of creation in Genesis? There was a definite pattern in God's work. God met every need of His creations before they needed it. When the fish and sea animals were created, the water was already waiting for them. When the land animals were made, there was food ready for them. When Adam and Eve were created, they stepped into a garden that had been prepared for them. God met every need before it was a need. He provided for His creation, and He still does.

After Adam and Eve were banished from the Garden of Eden, they had to work and toil for their food, but God still provided for them. He provided rain to make food grow. He gave them trees for wood to make shelter. We live in a fallen world, but God still provides for His people.

God knows what we need before we even ask. He knew what Adam and Eve would need before they took their first breath. God didn't wait for Adam's stomach to rumble before He provided food, the food was already there, waiting for Adam. God knows what you need, and He will provide for you. It may not always come the way we want, but His provision will be there.

As much as we focus on bills, financial obligations, and things we want to buy, God knows this isn't our deepest need. We need Him. We need God more than we need anything else. When we put Him first, we open the door for His blessings to flow in every other area of our lives. Our greatest need is to be in relationship with Jesus Christ, and God has met that need if we are willing to receive it.

As we go through this life, God wants to be our provider. He will meet our needs according to His timing and His purpose. It may not always be what we want, but it will always be what we need. Jesus taught us to pray, "Give us today our daily bread," (Matthew 6:11). God wants us to be dependent on Him, trusting in Him and not in ourselves for our provision. God is the source of our riches, and He has promised to be our provider. Our job is to daily trust in Him and put Him first.

Prayer For Today

FATHER GOD,

Thank you for providing for me. You have already met my greatest need in the sacrifice of Your Son for my salvation, and I know I can trust You with everything else. Be my provision, Lord. I will trust in You and depend on You for my daily bread. Help me choose each day to put You first.

Amen

"'Because he loves me,' says the Lord, 'I will rescue him; I will protect him, for he acknowledges my name.'"
Psalm 91:14

Once upon a time, a young girl was playing with her favorite ball. After a particularly big bounce, the ball rolled away from her. On and on it went, getting further out of her reach. Panicked, the girl chased after it. She nearly had it when her father grabbed her arm and yanked her back. Her ball was gone, and her heart was broken. She cried and cried, mourning the loss of her favorite toy, and demanding to know why her father had let it happen.

Sounds like a sad story, right? An unjust father robbing his child of the one thing she truly loved. Should we call the authorities? Should we tell the girl to run away, to turn her back on the father who had been so cruel to her?

What if I told you that the ball had rolled into the road? What if I told you the young girl was so focused on the ball that she didn't see the car heading toward her? And what if I told you that her father grabbed her and pulled her to safety, protecting her from the car?

Now the story is no longer about a cruel and uncaring father, but about a father who rescued his child and saved her from a danger she couldn't see.

God has promised to protect you. You are His child, and He loves you. God is at work protecting you from dangers you can't see. Many times, we are so focused on what we want, and how we feel when things don't go our way, that we forget there are battles raging that we know nothing about. We lose our ball and think God has forgotten us, that He doesn't care, or He isn't interested. We don't see the car that was heading for us, the danger that would have destroyed us, and we don't realize that the hand of God was upon us.

When something bad happens, we may think it is a sign that God hasn't been paying attention. We hear the word protection and think that means protection from everything, that nothing bad should ever happen to us. We expect God to stop every terrible, painful, or harmful thing that comes our way. And when something bad does happen, we assume that means God has abandoned us.

But we can't see the whole picture. We can only see the ball bouncing away from us. God sees the car. We will never know on this side of Heaven what God has defended us from, what wars He has waged on our behalf, and what devastation He has stopped.

God has promised to protect His people, and His word is true. Our feelings can mislead us. Our perception can be wrong. That is why we must decide in advance to trust God's word. Bad things will happen because we live in a fallen world. When trouble comes, trust that God doesn't lie. Believe that His promises are true. God is protecting you. He is your shield and your rear guard and He will never leave you.

Prayer For Today

MIGHTY GOD,

Thank you, Lord, for Your protection. Thank you for watching over me and keeping me safe. I believe that You are with me, and Your hand of protection is over me. I may not always see the battles You are fighting, but I trust that You are with me. You have promised to protect me and never leave me. Help me always trust that Your promises are true.

Amen

"Being strengthened with all power according to His glorious
might so that you may have great endurance and patience."
Colossians 1:11

*Y*ou are stronger than you think you are.

God has filled you with His power through the Holy Spirit, and it is His strength that flows within you. You do not have to face bad news alone. You do not have to endure a frightening diagnosis on your own. When your world falls apart, when you are faced with a nightmare you never thought would happen, you are stronger than you think you are because you are not alone. God's strength gives you the ability to keep going.

Over and over the Bible reminds us that God is our strength:

"God is our refuge and strength, an ever-present help in trouble" (Psalm 46:1).

"The Lord is my strength and my shield; my heart trusts in Him and He helps me" (Psalm 28:7).

"My flesh and my heart may fail, but God is the strength of my heart and my portion forever" (Psalm 73:26).

You do not have to rely on your own strength to face the trials of life because God has given you His strength.

After my husband retired from the Marine Corps, we settled in Southern California and bought a house. There was a young, scrawny, baby tree planted in the front yard. It was barely more than a stick with a few leaves on it. In a storm, it would tilt wildly, rocked back and forth by the winds. I wasn't convinced the tree would survive the winter. It was such a skinny thing and the winds were relentless.

Then a landscaper came out. He stuck two thick poles into the ground on either side of our baby tree and looped thick black bands around the poles and the trunk of the tree. Day after day the winds came, but the poles lent strength to the tree. They stood beside it, helping it stay upright. Those poles provided support and helped the tree withstand the winds. By the time spring came, the tree had not only survived, it had grown.

In a world that places so much emphasis on independence and self-reliance, it can be hard to ask for help. We are taught to do it on our own, to grin and bear it, to suck it up. As a Christian you don't have to face the winds of life alone. God is with you. He has given you His strength, and He wants to stand beside you, to help you endure and stand strong in the face of opposition. His strength is in you.

The key to drawing on God's strength is to surrender to Him. When we stop depending on our own ability, God fills us with His strength. It's divine irony that the more we surrender, the stronger we become. The more we rely on God, the more powerful we become because we stop operating in our own capabilities and start walking in His power and strength.

You are stronger than you think because you are not alone. God is your strength.

Prayer For Today

FATHER GOD,

When I am weak, remind me that You are my strength. When I am afraid, be my courage. When I am worried, be my peace. Fill me with Your strength and help me to stand up against the winds that try to knock me down. I surrender to You because Your strength is better than anything I can do on my own.

Amen

YOU ARE VALUABLE

"Consider the ravens: They do not sow or reap, they have no storeroom or barn; yet God feeds them. And how much more valuable you are than birds!"
Luke 12:24

Fort Knox is considered one of the most secure vaults in the world. It houses approximately 5,000 tons of gold worth over $261,000,000,000. It is located in the middle of a secure Army base. The security is so secret that not even Google can tell you exactly what security measures are in place. There are armed guards, electric fences, and minefields surrounding it. Visitors are not allowed anywhere near it. The gold inside is guarded, protected, and secured.

People have fought wars for gold, killed for it, schemed for it, stolen it, smuggled it, and given their lives in pursuit of it. Do you know what God does with gold? He paves the streets with it. Gold has no value to God. He uses priceless pearls to build the gates in Heaven. Precious stones line the foundations of His city. God does not value gold, gemstones, or riches, but He values you. People may fight for a single bar of gold. Jesus fights for you.

It's easy to feel unimportant in this busy world. To feel like one voice lost in the middle of a world filled with noise. But God says you matter.

You are important.

You are valuable.

You are so valuable, in fact, that God paid the ultimate price for you. The gold in Fort Knox might be worth billions and billions of dollars, but you are worth the life of Jesus Christ. You are so valuable to God that He gave His only Son for you. You cannot put a price on the love of God. There is no number than can quantify the blood of Jesus Christ. No billionaire can buy what God freely gave.

Your worth is not determined by how much money you make, what job you have, what kind of car your drive or how many people like your photo on social media. Your worth is determined by the One who created you. Your worth is set by the hands that formed you. Just as an artist sets the price for their creation, God knows how much you are worth, and He says you are worth dying for. Jesus gave His life to buy your freedom. He sacrificed himself for you, bled for you, and died for you. Your value cannot be measured by anything other than the life of Jesus Christ.

You are not worthless. You are not insignificant. You are not invisible, unimportant, or overlooked. You are treasured by God, cherished by Him, and valued by Him. You are so precious to Him that He gave up everything on the cross for you. Your value is not determined by anything this world says, your value has been set by God, and He has declared that you are priceless.

Prayer For Today

FATHER GOD,

Thank you for loving me. Thank you for telling me that I am special, treasured, and priceless. You gave Your Son for me and nothing can ever compare to that. My worth comes from You. My value comes from You. I will not listen to the lies of this world any longer. I trust what Your Word says, and Your Word says that I am priceless.

Amen

YOU ARE NOT FINISHED

"Being confident of this, that he who began a good work in you
will carry it on to completion until the day of Christ Jesus."
Philippians 1:6

You are a work in progress. Your new life began the day you accepted Jesus Christ as your Savior. You were rescued from the kingdom of darkness and became a citizen of Heaven. You were set free from the bondage of sin, the chains of your past were broken, and your eternity was secured. You are a child of God: chosen, precious, and loved. Everything changed the moment you allowed Christ into your heart. You were made new. You were given a fresh start, a clean slate, and called into God's kingdom.

But your journey isn't over.

There is nothing more you need to do to earn your salvation. That work was finished on the cross and completed in your heart when you accepted God's forgiveness. There is nothing more you can do to earn God's love. In this very moment, He loves you as much as He ever will. The fullness of His grace and love is yours. He is holding nothing back from you.

But there is still work to be done.

You are clay in the hands of a Master Potter. He is shaping and molding you every day. In His hands, you are becoming more like Christ. This process will continue until the day you stand before His throne and look upon the face of the One who made you and saved you.

Wherever you are right now, good or bad, brand-new Christian or elder saint, walking in maturity or clawing back from a mistake, God isn't finished with you. He has work for you to do and work to do in you. You are a work in progress; a work of art being polished, perfected, and sculpted into a masterpiece.

God has plans for you. Whether you are eight or eighty, He has a plan and a purpose for your life. You are never too old or too young to serve Him. You are never beyond His plans, and it is never too late.

It doesn't matter where you are or where you've been, God has more for you. Open your heart to Him and let Him teach you. You cannot out-learn, out-serve, or out-love God. He has more in store for you if you are willing to receive it.

Prayer For Today

MIGHTY GOD,

I believe that You are at work in my life. Continue to refine me, Lord. Mold me and shape me so I can be more like Jesus. Give me opportunities to serve You. Lead me, Lord, and I will follow. Teach me, Lord, and I will learn. Let me never be content to stay where I am, but draw me ever closer to You until the day I see You face-to-face.

Amen

DAY THIRTY

YOU ARE VICTORIOUS

"But thanks be to God! He gives us the victory through our Lord
Jesus Christ."
1 Corinthians 15:57

In the book of Genesis, the enemy, in the form of a
serpent, tempted Adam and Eve into sin. Their deci-
sion led to the fall of this world and separation from God, but
God did not give up on them. Though they disobeyed Him, hid
from Him, and allowed His perfect creation to be corrupted, He
did not turn His back on them. The consequences of their sin
have filtered down through the ages and left this world in
desperate need of rescue. But way back in that garden, God made
a way. He promised salvation. He promised a Redeemer that
would conquer sin and death.

That Redeemer came in His Son, Jesus Christ. The victory
over sin and death was won on the cross. As believers, we share
in that victory. Sin has no power over us, death has no power

over us, and the enemy of our souls has no power over us. We are victorious because of the shed blood of Jesus Christ. Though the battle rages on around us, we have already won. The victory is ours.

But we don't always feel victorious. Life is hard, bad things happen; we mess up, try again, and mess up again. It doesn't always feel like we've won. That's when we need to remember the truth, repeat it over and over, write it on a sticky note and put it on the mirror: The victory is won!

You are not barely making it, you are not scraping by, you are not limping your way through life. You are overwhelmingly victorious because of the love of Jesus Christ.

It's time to believe it and walk in it. That means applying the truth of God's Word and His promises to our lives. It's one thing to read about the truth, but it's another to live it. We must walk in the victory God has given us. Step-by-step and inch-by-inch, walking in the unwavering belief that the victory has been won. There is nothing to doubt, no room for second guessing. The battle may rage, and we may get caught in the crossfire, but that doesn't change the truth. God has won! Satan would love to convince you otherwise. He will try to get you to surrender, to give up what has already been won. Don't fall for it. He is a liar, and he has been crushed beneath the cross.

It's easy to start worrying and doubting if we sit on the sidelines of our faith. To be victorious, our faith must be active. We must apply it every day. Pray, read the Bible, turn on the worship music and crank it up loud. Surround yourself with evidence of God's power, His strength, His mercy, and yes, His victory. You are on the winning side. Jesus Christ is coming again with the armies of Heaven behind Him, and this world will be made new. He will reign in glory, and God Himself will be in the midst of His people. What was corrupt will be redeemed. What was lost will be found, and you will be a part of it. Praise the Lord for the victory He has won!

Prayer For Today

MIGHTY GOD,

You are victorious! You have defeated Hell, death, and the grave. You have triumphed. Your promises are true. Nothing can take what You have won. Help me walk in that victory. Help me remember that the battle is won, and I have a place in Heaven, an eternity in Your presence. Fill me, Lord, afresh with Your Holy Spirit so I can walk with boldness and confidence, knowing that the victory You won is mine to share. Nothing can defeat me because I belong to You.

Amen

I Am...Thirty Names God Has Given Himself and What They Mean

God is bigger than our greatest dreams and present in our smallest needs. In the Bible, God reveals Himself in His names.

Take a thirty day devotional journey into the names of God, what they mean, and how they can draw you closer to the God who loves you.

Mission Hollywood

A Hollywood bad boy. A pastor's daughter. What could possibly go wrong?

Rocked by sandal, his career in jeopardy, movie star Ben Prescott agrees to volunteer at a small Hollywood church. When he meets Lily Shaw, Ben must risk his career to follow his heart, but Lily wants the one thing he doesn't have: faith

Made in Hollywood

When a pastor's son saves her life, a prodigal daughter dares to believe in second chances.

Hannah left her family and her faith when she ran away to Hollywood. Abandoned and alone, she's lost hope, until the night Noah Shaw saves her life. When the shadows of her former life threaten to expose her past, she must chose between running or fighting for the new life she's built and the man she's grown to love.

CONNECT WITH MICHELLE

Michelle loves to hear from readers. You can connect with her on Twitter, Facebook, or Instagram @MKeenerWrites.

If you would like to stay updated on Michelle's books, are interested in joining a launch team, or would like to schedule Michelle as a speaker check out her website www.michellekeener.com

For information on bulk order discounts on *You Are...* or *I Am...* for your church, please email info@MichelleKeener.com